ideals®
THANKSGIVING

This is togetherness, sharing and living;
This is true happiness; this is Thanksgiving.

–Richie Tankersley

DISCARD

IDEALS PUBLICATIONS
NASHVILLE, TENNESSEE

TRADITIONS
Hal Borland

This is the traditional day to give thanks. Traditions, of course, are based on customs and beliefs transmitted from generation to generation. Those we observe at Thanksgiving are mostly rural—the turkey, the feast, the thankful prayer. And all with the generous land close about, a world of fields made fruitful by calloused hands. The thanks were for health and strength and independence.

Looking back now, in a land whose people are largely urban, the day may seem to have only token meaning. And yet, in its origins the word thank meant "think," and surely one day out of the year is not too much to think back and remember.

The day of thanks goes back to a little band of immigrants fighting a strange wilderness, painfully getting a foothold there. They had little enough to be thankful for, yet they were grateful for survival and hoped for better days beyond the winter that was closing in. They had faith and belief and even dreams, though those dreams could not encompass what has come after them.

So the traditions are as important as the thanks themselves. The symbols are not without meaning, for they rest on the land's own bounty, on work and achievement, on obligations as well as rights. Nobody has yet outmoded harvest, or plenty, or gratitude.

Thanksgiving is more than a feast. It always was. It is recognition of the providence, the work, the hope and dreams that are in our very blood and being. It is thanks for the traditions themselves.

Jenne Farm, South Reading, Vermont.
Photograph by Dietrich Leis Photography

The Landing of the Pilgrims

Felicia Dorothea Hemans

The breaking waves dashed high
On a stern and rock-bound coast,
And the woods against a stormy sky
Their giant branches tossed;

And the heavy night hung dark
The hills and waters o'er,
When a band of exiles moored their bark
On the wild New England shore.

Not as the conqueror comes,
They, the true-hearted, came;
Not with the roll of the stirring drums,
And the trumpet that sings of fame;

Not as the fleeing come,
In silence and in fear;
They shook the depths of the desert gloom
With their hymns of lofty cheer.

Amidst the storm they sang,
And the stars heard, and the sea;
And the sounding aisles of the dim woods rang
To the anthem of the free!

The ocean eagle soared
From his nest by the white wave's foam;
And the rocking pines of the forest roared—
This was their welcome home!

MAYFLOWER II, *Plymouth, Massachusetts.*
Photograph by Dietrich Leis Photography

Thanksgiving Day
Alice Williams Brotherton

Heap high the board with plenteous cheer
And gather to the feast.
And toast the sturdy Pilgrim band
Whose courage never ceased.
Give praise to that All-Gracious One
By whom their steps were led
And thanks unto the harvest's Lord
Who sends our daily bread.

THE FIRST THANKSGIVING
Autumn 1621

THE FIRST THANKSGIVING. *Painting by Jean Leon Gerome Ferris*

OUR HARVEST BEING GOTTEN IN, our governor sent four men on fowling, that so we might, after a special manner, rejoice together after we had gathered the fruits of our labors. They four in one day killed as much fowl as, with a little help beside, served the company almost a week.

At which time, among other recreations, we exercised our arms, many of the Indians coming among us, and among the rest their greatest king, Massasoit, with some ninety men, whom for three days we entertained and feasted; and they went out and killed five deer, which they brought to the plantation and bestowed on our governor and upon the captain and others. And although it be not always so plentiful as it was at this time with us, yet by the goodness of God we are so far from want, that we often wish you partakers of our plenty.

—Edward Winslow, MOURT'S RELATION

AND THUS, THEY FOUND THE LORD to be with them in all their ways, and to bless their outgoings and incomings, for which let His holy name have the praise forever, to all posterity.

They began now to gather in the small harvest they had, and to fit up their houses and dwellings against winter, being all well recovered in health and strength, and had all things in good plenty. For as some were thus employed in affairs abroad, others were exercised in fishing, about cod and bass and other fish, of which they took good store, of which every family had their portion.

All the summer there was no want; and now began to come in store of fowl, as winter aproached, of which this place did abound when they came first (but afterward decreased by degrees). And besides waterfowl, there was great store of wild turkeys, of which they took many, besides venison, etc. Besides, they had about a peck of meal a week to a person, or now since harvest, Indian corn to that proportion. Which made many afterwards write so largely of their plenty here to their friends in England, which were not feigned, but true reports.

—William Bradford, OF PLYMOUTH PLANTATION

A City Upon a Hill

John Winthrop

We are a company professing ourselves fellow members of Christ, in which respect only though we were absent from each other many miles and had our employments as far distant, yet we ought to account ourselves knit together by this bond of love and live in the exercise of it, if we would have comfort of our being in Christ. . . .

The end is to improve our lives to do more service to the Lord; the comfort and increase of the body of Christ, whereof we are members; that ourselves and posterity may be the better preserved from the common corruptions of this evil world, to serve the Lord and work out our salvation under the power and purity of His holy ordinances. . . .

The Lord will be our God and delight to dwell among us, as His own people, and will command a blessing upon us in all our ways, so that we shall see much more of His wisdom, power, goodness, and truth, than formerly we have been acquainted with. We shall find that the God of Israel is among us when ten of us shall be able to resist a thousand of our enemies; when He shall make us a praise and glory that men shall say of succeeding plantations, "the Lord make it like that of New England."

For we must consider that we shall be as a

city upon a hill. The eyes of all people are upon us so that if we shall deal falsely with our God in this work we have undertaken, and so cause Him to withdraw His present help from us, we shall be made a story and a byword through the world. . . . We shall shame the faces of many of God's worthy servants and cause their prayers to be turned into curses upon us till we be consumed out of the good land whither we are going. . . .

Beloved, there is now set before us life and good, death and evil, in that we are commanded this day to love the Lord our God, and to love one another, to walk in His ways, and to keep His commandments and His ordinance and His laws and the articles of our covenant with Him, that we may live and be multiplied and that our Lord our God may bless us in the land whither we go to possess it.

But if our hearts shall turn away, so that we will not obey, but shall be seduced and worship other gods, our pleasures and profits, and serve them; it is propounded unto us this day, we shall surely perish out of the good land whither we pass over this vast sea to possess it.

Therefore let us choose life, that we and our seed may live by obeying His voice and cleaving to Him, for He is our life and our prosperity.

Sanbornton Square, Sanbornton, Hew Hampshire.
Photograph by William H. Johnson

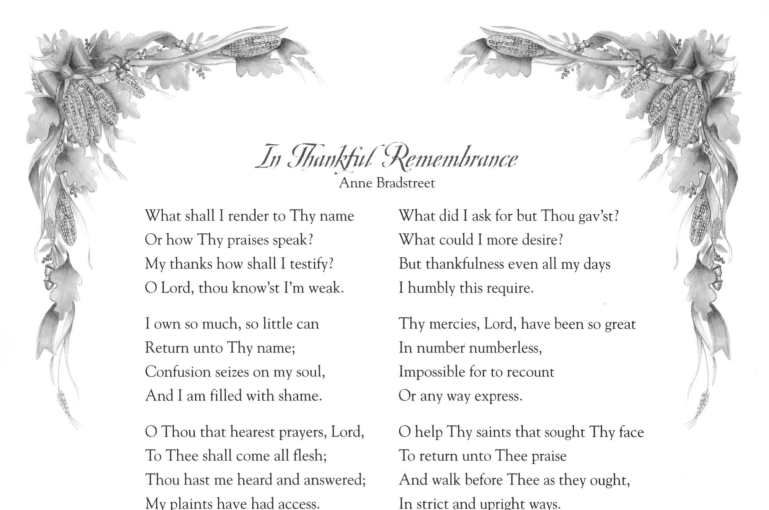

In Thankful Remembrance
Anne Bradstreet

What shall I render to Thy name
Or how Thy praises speak?
My thanks how shall I testify?
O Lord, thou know'st I'm weak.

I own so much, so little can
Return unto Thy name;
Confusion seizes on my soul,
And I am filled with shame.

O Thou that hearest prayers, Lord,
To Thee shall come all flesh;
Thou hast me heard and answered;
My plaints have had access.

What did I ask for but Thou gav'st?
What could I more desire?
But thankfulness even all my days
I humbly this require.

Thy mercies, Lord, have been so great
In number numberless,
Impossible for to recount
Or any way express.

O help Thy saints that sought Thy face
To return unto Thee praise
And walk before Thee as they ought,
In strict and upright ways.

A NATIONAL PRAYER
Thomas Jefferson

Almighty God, who has given us this good land for our heritage, we humbly beseech Thee that we may always prove ourselves a people mindful of Thy favor and glad to do Thy will.

Bless our land with honorable industry, sound learning, and pure manners. Save us from violence, discord, and confusion, from pride and arrogance, and from every evil way. Defend our liberties and fashion into one united people the multitude brought hither out of many kindreds and tongues.

Endow with the spirit of wisdom those to whom in Thy name we entrust the authority of government that there may be justice and peace at home and, that through obedience to Thy law, we may show forth Thy praise among the nations of the earth.

In time of prosperity, fill our hearts with thankfulness, and, in the day of trouble, suffer not our trust in Thee to fail; all of which we ask through Jesus Christ our Lord. Amen.

Blueberry field on Caterpillar Hill, Hancock County, Maine.
Photograph by Donnelly Austin Photography

A New England Thanksgiving

Juliana Smith

This year it was Uncle Simeon's turn to have the dinner at his house, but of course we all helped them as they help us when it is our turn, and there is always enough for us all to do. All the baking of pies and cakes was done at our house, and we had the big oven heated and filled twice each day for three days before it was all done, and everything was good, though we did have to do without some things that ought to be used.

There was no Plum Pudding, but a boiled Suet Pudding, stirred thick with dried Plums and Cherries, was called by the old Name and answered the purpose. All the other spice had been used in the Mince Pies, so for this Pudding we used a jar of West India preserved Ginger which chanced to be left of the last shipment which Uncle Simeon had from there. We chopped the Ginger small and stirred it through with the Plums and Cherries. It was extraordinarily good.

The Day was bitter cold and when we got home from Meeting, which Father did not keep over long by reason of the cold, we were glad eno' of the fire in Uncle's Dining Hall; but by the time the dinner was one-half over, those of us who were on the fire side of one Table were forced to get up and carry our

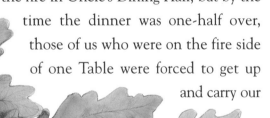

plates with us around to the far side of the other Table, while those who had sat there were glad to bring their plates around to the fire side to get warm. All but the Old Ladies who had a screen put behind their chairs.

Uncle Simeon was in his best mood, and you know how good that is! He kept both Tables in a roar of laughter with his droll stories of the days when he was studying medicine in Edinburgh, and afterwards he and Father and Uncle Paul joined in singing Hymns and Ballads. You know how fine their voices go together. Then we all sang a Hymn, and afterwards my dear Father led us in prayer, remembering all Absent Friends before the Throne of Grace, and much I wished that my dear Betsey was here as one of us, as she has been of yore.

We did not rise from the Table until it was quite dark, and then when the dishes had been cleared away we all got round the fire as close as we could and cracked nuts and sang songs and told stories. At least some told and others listened. You know nobody can exceed the two Grandmothers at telling tales of all the things they have seen themselves and repeating those of the early years in New England, and even some in the Old England, which they had heard in their youth from their Elders. My Father says it is a goodly custom to hand down all worthy deeds and traditions from Father to Son, as the Israelites were commanded to do about Passover and as the Indians here have always done because the Word that is spoken is remembered longer than the one that is written.

Cornucopia. Photograph by Ideals Publications

So once in every year we throng
    Upon a day apart
To praise the Lord with feast and song
    In thankfulness of heart.
            —ARTHUR GUITERMAN

A Thanksgiving Proclamation

Abraham Lincoln

The year that is drawing towards its close has been filled with the blessings of fruitful fields and healthful skies. To these bounties, which are so constantly enjoyed that we are prone to forget the source from which they come, others have been added, which are of so extraordinary a nature that they cannot fail to penetrate and soften even the heart which is habitually insensible to the ever watchful providence of Almighty God. . . .

No human counsel hath devised nor hath any mortal hand worked out these great things. They are the gracious gifts of the Most High God, who, while dealing with us in anger for our sins, hath nevertheless remembered mercy.

It has seemed to me fit and proper that they should be solemnly, reverently, and gratefully acknowledged as with one heart and voice by the whole American People. I do, therefore, invite my fellow citizens in every part of the United States, and also those who are at sea and those who are sojourning in foreign lands, to set apart and observe the last Thursday of November next, as a day of Thanksgiving and Praise to our beneficent Father who dwelleth in the Heavens.

And I recommend to them that while offering up the ascriptions justly due to Him for such singular deliverances and blessings, they do also, with humble penitence for our national perverseness and disobedience, commend to His tender care all those who have become widows, orphans, mourners, or sufferers in the lamentable civil strife in which we are unavoidably engaged, and fervently implore the interposition of the Almighty Hand to heal the wounds of the nation and to restore it as soon as may be consistent with the Divine purposes to the full enjoyment of peace, harmony, tranquillity, and Union.

The First Turkey Pardon

During Abraham Lincoln's presidency, a turkey was presented to the White House as part of the menu for a holiday dinner. Tad, the Lincolns' youngest son, adopted the bird as a pet and walked it around the White House grounds. Upon learning that the turkey was about to be dispatched for dinner, Tad interrupted his father's cabinet meeting to protest the turkey's demise. President Lincoln wrote a note giving an official pardon for Tad to present to the "executioner." And thus began an American tradition of presidential pardons for turkeys at Thanksgiving.

Pomfret, Vermont. Photograph by Dietrich Leis Photography

A MASSACHUSETTS PROCLAMATION

Harriet Beecher Stowe

When the apples were all gathered, and the cider was all made, and the yellow pumpkins were rolled in from many a hill in billows of gold, and the corn was husked, and the labors of the season were done, and the warm, late days of Indian summer came in, dreamy and calm and still, with just frost enough to crisp the ground of a morning, but with warm trances of benignant, sunny hours at noon, there came over the community a sort of genial repose of spirit—a sense of something accomplished, and of a new golden mark made in advance on the calendar of life— and the deacon began to say to the minister, of a Sunday, "I suppose it's about time for the Thanksgiving proclamation." . . .

The glories of that proclamation! We knew beforehand the Sunday it was to be read and walked to church with alacrity, filled with gorgeous and vague expectations.

The cheering anticipation sustained us through what seemed to us the long waste of the sermon and prayers; and when at last the auspicious moment approached—when the last quaver of the last hymn had died out—the whole house rippled with a general movement of complacency, and a satisfied smile of pleased expectation might be seen gleaming on the faces of all the young people, like a ray of sunshine through a garden of flowers.

Thanksgiving now was dawning! We children poked one another and fairly giggled with unreproved delight as we listened to the crackle of the slowly unfolding document. That great sheet of paper impressed us as something supernatural, by reason of its mighty size and by the broad seal of the state affixed thereto; and when the minister read therefrom, "By his Excellency, the Governor of the Commonwealth of Massachusetts, a Proclamation," our mirth was with difficulty repressed by glances from our sympathetic elders.

Then, after a solemn enumeration of the benefits which the Commonwealth had that year received at the hands of Divine Providence, came at last the naming of the eventful day, and, at the end of all, the imposing heraldic words, "God save the Commonwealth of Massachusetts." And then, as the congregation broke up and dispersed, all went their several ways with schemes of mirth and feasting in their heads.

Old Meeting House, Sugar Hill, New Hampshire.
Photograph by Dietrich Leis Photography

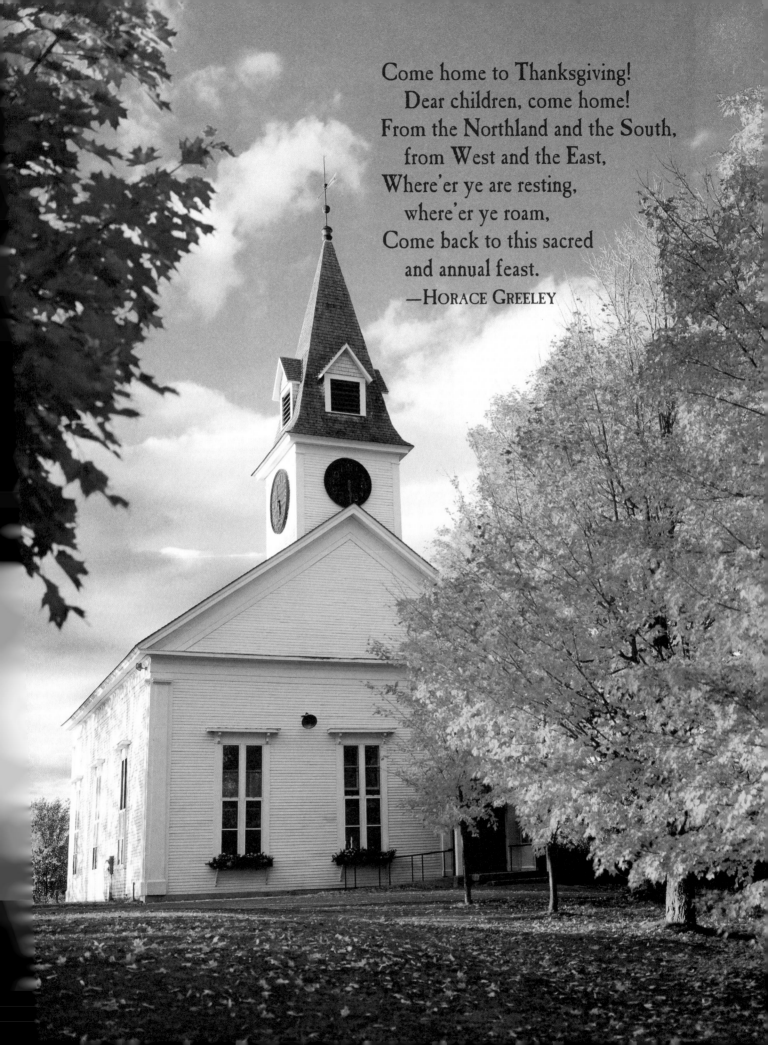

Come home to Thanksgiving!
Dear children, come home!
From the Northland and the South,
from West and the East,
Where'er ye are resting,
where'er ye roam,
Come back to this sacred
and annual feast.
—HORACE GREELEY

A Morning of Thanksgiving

Lansing Christman

I awoke to a new world a few mornings ago, the first frost, a heavy one that transformed the countryside into a crystalline loveliness. It was a pure, rich morning of reverent meditation, truly a morning of Thanksgiving.

Pastures and fields and roadsides were snow-white. So were the roofs of houses and barns. It was a sparkling morning of dazzling beauty when the sun peered over the eastern horizon. Night had slipped millions of diamonds on the fingers of grass and weeds. She had looped strings of pearls around the neck of the hills.

The time always comes when the late flowers and gardens feel the stinging needles of the frost. It claims the kudzu vines climbing banks and trees and nips the soft pink flowers of the oxalis. The Earth drowses and nods as Autumn closes the shutters on her house.

Nothing can halt the cycle that brings one season on the heels of another. Each season

comes on its own terms and on its own schedule. The sun tells us that.

The first morning of frost brought flocks of robins to the dogwood trees in the yard. The trees were loaded with berries of scarlet and red that glistened in the sheen of the new day's sun. Within an hour, the berries were gone. And so were the robins.

That morning was Thanksgiving for the robins. My yard was their dining room; the dogwoods were the tables from which they dined.

It was Thanksgiving for me too, for that matter. It was an inspiring morning, a reason to be thankful for a natural environment that brings the birds to my door with their songs and carols. It brings them in spring to nest in the bushes and trees and in winter to the dooryard feeders.

The leaves on the dogwood have fallen, and the berries are gone. But I still have the birds around me. I hear the liquid warble of bluebirds playing house as they inspect the bird boxes in which they reared their young last spring. I hear the sweet calls of the chickadees; and down in the woods, the bluejays and crows are calling.

And listen . . . there's the concert of the mockingbird in the dooryard holly tree.

Shelburne, Massachusetts. Photograph by William H. Johnson

Merry Autumn
Paul Laurence Dunbar

It's all a farce—these tales they tell
    About the breezes sighing
And moans astir o'er field and dell
    Because the year is dying.

Such principles are most absurd—
    I care not who first taught 'em;
There's nothing known to beast or bird
    To make a solemn autumn.

Now purple tints are all around;
    The sky is blue and mellow;
And e'en the grasses turn the ground
    From modest green to yellow.

A butterfly goes winging by;
    A singing bird comes after;
And Nature, all from earth to sky,
    Is bubbling o'er with laughter.

The ripples wimple on the rills,
    Like sparkling little lasses;
The sunlight runs along the hills
    And laughs among the grasses.

The earth is just so full of fun,
    It really can't contain it;
And streams of mirth so freely run,
    The heavens seem to rain it.

Don't talk to me of solemn days
    In autumn's time of splendor
Because the sun shows fewer rays,
    And these grow slant and slender.

Why, it's the climax of the year—
    The highest time of living—
Till naturally its bursting cheer
    Just melts into Thanksgiving.

HARVEST QUILTS. *Painting by Diane Phalen*

THE GREAT GOBBLER GALLOP

Raymond Crippen

If we could find—if we could read—"The Chronicles of the Turkeys," amid myriad woeful stories of November martyrs and November massacres, there probably are warm and grateful accounts of turkey experiences at Worthington, Minnesota, and Cuero, Texas.

Oh, true, Worthington and Cuero have involved themselves in turkey slaughters. There is no denying this. But Worthington and Cuero also are believed to be the only two communities in America which have taught and coaxed and worked tirelessly to teach turkeys to run.

Cuero is host city for the annual Turkeyfest, a celebration of the awesome American turkey which has extended through ninety-eight years. Worthington is host city for Turkey Days, a similar community festival which began in 1939.

Cuero's race contender, always a turkey named Ruby Begonia, is pitted against Worthington's bird, always named Paycheck.

The species name of the wild turkey is *Meleagris gallopavo*. Gallopavo. So it is each year, at their separate festivals, Worthington and Cuero conduct a Great Gobbler Gallop to determine who will carry home the Traveling Trophy of Tumultuous Triumph. Cuero's race contender, always a turkey named Ruby Begonia, is pitted against Worthington's bird, always named Paycheck. (Nothing goes faster than a Paycheck.)

The birds race first along Worthington's main street. There is a second, deciding heat along Cuero's main street.

The turkeys are expected and instructed to run. Any American who has partaken of a Thanksgiving dinner is aware, however, that turkeys have wings. Ruby Begonia and Paycheck often take to flight, soaring over the throngs that cheer them on. Time spent getting contenders back on the racetrack is time lost and, usually, this means the race is lost.

America's news and entertainment media have taken to tagging the nation's annual Thanksgiving observance, "Turkey Day." This has a hollow ring in Minnesota and in Texas where actual Turkey Days are both festivals and traditions.

What happens at Turkey Day, at Turkeyfest? Both are just a lot of fun. The first unit of the first Turkey Day parade at Worthington nearly seventy years gone by set the tone for the celebration: Benny Palmer had a tickling idea. Benny made a miniature buggy with four spoked wheels. Next he fashioned what appeared to be a pair of Munchkin legs inside tight blue jeans and cowboy boots. He propped the little legs in front of his buggy seat. Finally, Benny hitched a pair of tom turkeys to his mini-wagon and lowered his own long legs through a hole in the seat. Although Benny was walking, providing man power, it appeared Benny, with tiny legs, was being drawn along the avenue by his team of tom turkeys.

Everyone laughed. *Life* magazine printed a picture of Benny Palmer and his turkey buggy.

Once there were great flocks of turkeys on the prairie farms of both Texas and Minnesota. There were turkey hatcheries and turkey processing plants. Turkeys were an industry, and Worthington fancied itself to be the earth's Turkey Capital.

The evidence of turkeys at Worthington is scant by now but a soft claim can be made that no people anywhere have celebrated turkeys with greater fervor, or with more free pancakes, or with more marching bands. This is a "soft claim" because Cuero has an identical turkey heritage. Its people also celebrate the centerpiece of Thanksgiving dinners with laughter, good food, and brass bands.

Someone said, "I never heard of Turkey Day." From that time when major political candidates still made appearances across rural America, Worthington's Turkey Day gained fame from a succession of celebrated speakers, among them Lyndon Johnson, who was soaked by a rain storm; Richard Nixon; Robert Kennedy, who attracted a crowd estimated at fifty thousand people; Nelson Rockefeller, Jesse Jackson and, most often, Minnesota's erstwhile favorite sons, Walter Mondale and Hubert Humphrey.

Turkey Day parades are led by a flock of marching turkeys. That was one of the things that delighted Hubert Humphrey. He laughed whenever he saw them, and he saw them often. He attended Turkey Day celebrations even when he had no role as parade marshal or featured speaker. He never missed a Turkey Day in an election year—he won every election.

Alas. In 1968, when he campaigned for the White House, Humphrey missed being at Worthington's Turkey Day. Like Paycheck that year, he lost his race.

Wild turkeys. Photograph by SuperStock

A Day for Parades

Robert M. Grippo

Each and every one of us has a favorite holiday. For some, nothing can beat Christmas Day or perhaps the Fourth of July. For me, my favorite holiday was and still is Thanksgiving Day. Thanksgiving is not only a day for family and friends to get together to give thanks for all their blessings, but also a day for ushering in the holiday season with a celebration of floats, clowns, marching bands, celebrities, and, of course, balloons some seventy feet tall in the shape of cartoon characters of yesterday and today.

Thanksgiving Day in our house had its own ritual. We rose at the crack of dawn as Mom prepared the turkey for the anticipated meal, and then we took a choice position in the living room to watch the big event on television: the Macy's Thanksgiving Day Parade. As the heavenly aroma of the cooking turkey engulfed the house, we watched the giant Bullwinkle, Underdog, Mickey Mouse, Smokey the Bear, and Superman balloons as they cast shadows along the granite jungle. We were transfixed.

Through the years, countless millions of people of all ages have lined the streets in rain, sleet, and snow to unite in one mass of holiday delight.

From its humble beginnings in 1924 through its present-day annual trek down the streets of Manhattan, the parade has entertained with a style all its own, a style different from any other parade. With its signature balloons and celebrity-decked floats, the parade has always welcomed the one and only Santa Claus to New York City.

Introduction from Macy's Thanksgiving Day Parade, *by Robert M. Grippo and Christopher Hoskins/Arcadia Publishing*

A parade makes us all feel childlike delight again.
—John Aiken

Macy's Thanksgiving Day Parade.
Photograph by SuperStock

A DAY FOR GAMES

Marjorie Lloyd

I don't know what it is about the Thanksgiving game. Maybe it's the holiday or that it's on national television, but there's magic in that game for the Lions.— Keith Dorney, former Detroit Lions' offensive lineman

The inclusion of a football game in the festivities of Thanksgiving Day has settled comfortably into an American tradition. For some families, gathering around a television to watch the Dallas Cowboys or the Detroit Lions is almost as important as the second helping of turkey and dressing. Everyone clusters into a loudly vocal group, and differences in politics, finances, and ages are forgotten as hands slap other hands with victorious exclamations, or as complex analyses of defeat are discussed in hushed tones.

Attending football games on Thanksgiving Day has been a longstanding event for Americans for more than one hundred years. From as early as the late 1800s, universities have played games with overflowing crowds on Thanksgiving Day. In 1882, the *New York Times* reported that residents of New York City were astonished by shouts and yells and the clattering of four-horse hotel coaches, filled with college students, as they raced to the Polo Grounds for the football game between Yale and Princeton.

High school playoff games on Thanksgiving Day are also an important family excursion, especially if a member of the family is on a team. Even NFL professional Doug Flutie has stated his high school game on Thanksgiving Day has always been the highlight of his football career.

But my fondest memories of football on Thanksgiving Day are the more informal contests played on our lawn after Thanksgiving dinner with teams made up of a few adults, cousins of various ages, and sometimes other teenagers from our neighborhood. The lineup changed with each play as Rick, the most athletic cousin, would swap teams in order to help keep the score more even. We gleefully plotted our strategy, cheered on by the toddlers and sometimes mothers who would sit briefly on the porch steps. The

Wabeno, Wisconsin. Photograph by Darryl R. Beers

final score was always hotly debated but eventually agreed upon, and we then went back into the house for more slices of pumpkin pie and mint-flavored tea, with the winners first in line.

My friends and cousins and other families across the United States who have enjoyed watching football games or playing an informal touch game amid cushiony leaf piles are really not so different from the people at the first Thanksgiving festival. In the fall of 1621, the Pilgrim children played games like "ring and pin," a type of horseshoes, and an early version of blind-man's bluff. The adults, including the Wampanoag who had befriended the Pilgrims, competed in demonstrations of musket shooting and archery skills.

It would seem that one of our most popular traditions, along with the turkey and cranberry sauce, is friendly competition. Perhaps the pleasure is in breathing the crisp, fresh air of an autumn afternoon, knowing that winter may arrive tomorrow; or maybe it is just in the simple chance to run and then roll on the ground with laughter flowing on all sides, knowing that the one who just knocked you down will also extend a hand to help you up.

Home Again
Gelia K. Parker

I return to this place for Thanksgiving,
Hills created with scarlet and gold,
And hear whispered from treetop to treetop
The nostalgic memories they hold.

Goin' Home
Edna Jaques

Goin' home—what lovelier word
Ever, ever, could be heard—
Home to warmth and firelight,
Little rooms that shine at night,
Back to the comfort of old things,
A kitchen where a kettle sings.

Goin' home—to supper spread,
Fried potatoes and homemade bread,
Slippers warm beside the hearth,
Loveliest spot in all the earth,
A new book, and an easy chair,
Someone precious waiting there.

Goin' home—to the place you've made
With your own hands that you wouldn't trade
For a palace on a golden hill,
Where you've sweated and planned until
Every tree in the rooted soil
Is yours by dint of patient toil.

Goin' home—with heart aglow,
Down the old road white with snow,
There a lighted window gleams,
Sending out its golden beams
Like a lighthouse tall and white,
Shining out against the night.

Greenbanks Hollow Covered Bridge, Danville, Vermont.
Photograph by William H. Johnson

AN OLD-FASHIONED THANKSGIVING

Louisa May Alcott

November had come; the crops were in; and barn, buttery, and bin were overflowing with the harvest that rewarded the summer's hard work.

The big kitchen was a jolly place just now, for in the great fireplace roared a cheerful fire; on the walls hung garlands of dried apples, onions, and corn; up aloft from the beams shone crook-necked squashes, juicy hams, and dried venison—for in those days deer still haunted the deep forests, and hunters flourished. Savory smells were in the air; on the crane hung steaming kettles, and down among the red embers copper saucepans simmered, all suggestive of some approaching feast.

Thanksgiving Day in the Morning

Aileen Fisher

What is the place you like the best,
Thanksgiving Day in the morning?
The kitchen! With so many things to test,
And help to measure, and stir with zest,
And sniff, and sample, and all the rest—
Thanksgiving Day in the morning.

What are the colors you like the most,
Thanksgiving Day in the morning?
The color of cranberries uppermost,
The pumpkin-yellow the pie-tops boast,
The turkey-brown of a crispy roast—
Thanksgiving Day in the morning.

What are the sounds you think are gay,
Thanksgiving Day in the morning?
The sizzly pops on the roaster-tray,
The gravy bubbling itself away,
The company knocks at the door—hooray!
Thanksgiving Day in the morning.

Country kitchen. Photograph by Jessie Walker

The Old-Fashioned Thanksgiving
Edgar A. Guest

It may be I am getting old and like too much to dwell
Upon the days of bygone years, the days I loved so well.
But thinking of them now I wish somehow that I could know
A simple old Thanksgiving Day, like those of long ago,
When all the family gathered round a table richly spread,
With little Jamie at the foot and Grandpa at the head,
The youngest of us all to greet the oldest with a smile,
With mother running in and out and laughing all the while.

I like the olden way the best, when relatives were glad
To meet the way they used to do when I was but a lad;
The old home was a rendezvous for all our kith and kin,
And whether living far or near they all came trooping in
With shouts of "Hello, Daddy!" as they fairly stormed the place
And made a rush for Mother, who would stop to wipe her face
Upon her gingham apron before she kissed them all,
Hugging them proudly to her breast, the grownups and the small.

Then laughter rang throughout the home, and, oh, the jokes they told;
From Boston, Frank brought new ones, but Father sprang the old.
All afternoon we chatted, telling what we hoped to do,
The struggles we were making, and the hardships we'd gone through.
We gathered round the fireside; how fast the hours would fly—
It seemed before we'd settled down 'twas time to say goodbye.
Those were the glad Thanksgivings the old-time families knew,
When relatives could still be friends and every heart was true.

The Historical Society House, Center Sandwich, New Hampshire.
Photograph by William H. Johnson

THANKSGIVING ON THE FARM

Helen M. Oakley

Everywhere is the anticipation of Thanksgiving Day. The churches are having special services. The school hallways are filled with drawings of turkeys, cornstalks, pumpkins, and the horn of plenty overflowing with fruits, vegetables, and nuts. Dried corn and stalks are made into decorations for front doors. Friends and relatives are guests in just about every house in the community—many are spending the entire Thanksgiving holiday, Wednesday through Sunday.

Mother has been selecting choice tomatoes to keep for a salad on Thanksgiving Day—she makes daily trips to the garden to gather them when they are just right. She has also been setting aside the

---

Pumpkin, apple, and mince pies are stacked on the racks, and cranberries are bubbling on the back of the stove.

---

best squash, smoothest carrots, and a beautiful green cabbage and storing them in the cellar with the winter potatoes and apples. Father always says, "A full cellar is a must on the farm, as there is no telling what winter will bring."

The boys have been searching for hickory nuts in the woods so that Mother can make her delicious nut cake. The girls bring small jars of jellies and jams. By now, the cupboard shelves are filled with pickles, relishes, and dried fruits and nuts. Into the freezer go packages of brown bread and mincemeat cookies. The day before the holiday, Mother makes her famous pumpkin pies with eggs, fresh pumpkin, spices, sugar, and creamy milk from the milk house.

At dawn on Thanksgiving Day, everyone meets at the Blueberry Farm for breakfast. Then, the turkey is filled with old-fashioned stuffing made of sage, dried breadcrumbs, onion, chopped celery, and broth. Father helps to place the heavy turkey into the oven.

Pumpkin, apple, and mince pies are stacked on the racks, and cranberries are bubbling on the back of the stove. Brown sugar beans are cooking in the pot, and Mother is getting ready to pop some baking powder biscuits into another oven. A large hubbard squash is almost done, and Father will scrape the pulp into a large bowl, then mix in butter. Grandmother says there must be a hubbard squash or it isn't a proper Thanksgiving dinner.

After we all crowd around the table and begin to enjoy our favorite dishes, conversation turns to Thanksgiving Days gone by. Father recalls, when he was a boy, the faint tinkle of sleigh bells as many guests approached his grandparents' house in the country. A guest recalls the singing tea kettle on her grandmother's black cooking stove and the full wood box nearby. Another guest remembers that she had Thanksgiving dinner at her aunt's house, with a large pot of wild game and all the "fixin's" anyone could hold.

As I listen to them, I know these are the special days, the good times that will be cherished and recalled on many Thanksgivings to come.

Mother says, "This is a happy Thanksgiving Day; may we have many more."

A Thanksgiving Day breakfast table.
Photograph by Jessie Walker

Ah! on Thanksgiving Day,
   when from East and from West,
From North and from South
   came the pilgrim and guest. . . .
What moistens the lip
   and what brightens the eye?
What calls back the past
   like the rich pumpkin pie?
—JOHN GREENLEAF WHITTIER

THE THANKSGIVING TURKEY

Hal Borland

That big, colorful, and meaty bird which makes the table annually festive for America's traditional Thanksgiving is surrounded by strange and contradictory legends.

It is an American native, unknown elsewhere until the sixteenth century. It is generally believed that the name "turkey" came from the early discoverers' belief that the America they found was Asia; but logically, even under that misapprehension, the bird should have been called a Cathay hen. Confusion persisted when it received its scientific name, *Meleagris*. *Meleagris* literally mans "guinea hen," a bird with no relation to the turkey.

The natives of Mexico and the Southwest had domesticated the turkey long before the Spaniards came, but in the Southwest it was grown for its feathers, not its flesh. The Spaniards took turkeys back to Spain, and thence they were distributed throughout Europe.

Early English settlers brought turkeys to New England, only to find the woods full of wild turkeys. Later, when a national bird was being chosen, Ben Franklin and others urged the turkey for that honor. They lost the fight to the bald eagle.

The wild turkey, the deer, and the buffalo sustained most of the pioneers as the frontier moved west. And the turkey, deprived of formal honors, eventually ran away with the November holiday. Even there it comes to an ironic fate, colorful with cranberries, savory with sage, tasty with stuffing and gravy and mashed potatoes and, if you will, onions and turnips, mincemeat and pumpkin. The turkey, the all-American bird, provider of feathers and feasts, misnamed and imported to the land of its origins, symbol now of Thanksgiving.

Long may the turkey gobble!

The turkey is . . . a true original Native of America. . . . He is besides, though a little vain and silly, a bird of courage, and would not hesitate to attack a Grenadier of the British Guards who should presume to invade his farm yard with a red coat on.
—BENJAMIN FRANKLIN

PRIDE OF AUTUMN. *Painting by George Hinke*

Thanksgiving

Edgar A. Guest

Getting together to smile and rejoice;
And eating and laughing with folks of your choice;
And kissing the girls and declaring that they
Are growing more beautiful day after day;
Chatting and bragging a bit with the men;
Building the old family circle again;
Living the wholesome and old-fashioned cheer,
Just for awhile at the end of the year.

Greetings fly fast as we crowd through the door
And under the old roof we gather once more,
Just as we did when the youngsters were small;
Mother's a little bit grayer, that's all.
Father's a little bit older, but still
Ready to romp and to laugh with a will.
Here we are back at the table again
Telling our stories as women and men.

Bowed are our heads for a moment in prayer;
Oh, but we're grateful and glad to be there.
Home from the east land and home from the west,
Home with the folks that are dearest and best.
Out of the sham of the cities afar
We've come for a time to be just what we are.
Here we can talk of ourselves and be frank,
Forgetting position and station and rank.

Give me the end of the year and its fun,
When most of the planning and toiling is done;
Bring all the wanderers home to the nest;
Let me sit down with the ones I love best,
Hear the old voices still ringing with song,
See the old faces unblemished by wrong,
See the old table with all of its chairs;
And I'll put soul in my Thanksgiving prayers.

Historic Astor District, Green Bay, Wisconsin.
Photograph by Darryl R. Beers

THANKSGIVING

Marjorie Holmes

It's good to be a woman when your husband and your sons come home from the supermarket, staggering under Thanksgiving provender: candy, cheeses, celery leafing from a sack, fresh pineapple, great net bags of apples and oranges.

The kitchen is a wild clutter of pots and pans and mixing bowls. Little boys hover, snitching samples—a hunk of sticky mincemeat, handfuls of nuts and raisins, a finger lick of the spicy pumpkin you're striving to pour into a pie shell. Little girls clamber on kitchen stools to "help" by stirring and spilling and vigorously shaking flour sifters.

Little boys hover, snitching samples—a hunk of sticky mincemeat, handfuls of nuts and raisins, a finger lick of the spicy pumpkin you're striving to pour into a pie shell.

Cranberries bounce into a pan. They make a sound of toy bullets popping as they boil. Children beg to be lifted up to see.

Your husband makes a triumphal entry with the turkey, and the rite of preparing it begins. There is the old-fashioned, country-kitchen smell of singed pinfeathers. You scrub the white firm flesh until is as clean as the baby's skin.

It is traditional that he prepare the dressing, practically a tradition that he can't find the recipe. Finally, he assembles the ingredients with the fussy concern of a Waldorf chef. You rejoice to contribute the sack of dry bread you can never bear to throw out, but never know quite what to do with. Soon the rich odors of sage and onions flavor the air.

You collaborate on the trussing, the anointing with oil, the binding of the wings. Now into the old family faithful, the speckled roaster, and out to the chill back porch, to await its baking hour.

You sleep late, have a lazy breakfast, then rush to get everybody ready for church. You return spiritually refreshed from this gathering with others, which gives focus and meaning to this whole festival of blessings.

The fire feels good after the tingling outdoor air. Your husband mixes a fruity punch. Children dart in and out, to the reechoing order of "Shut the door!" They present you with a bulging sack of pinecones for a centerpiece and a spray of berries no rosier than their noses. A teenager shoos them from underfoot as she helps you open wide the table and spread it with your longest, loveliest cloth.

The fire dances. The wind rattles a shutter. Your big black Labrador growls and cocks a troubled ear. The mad and merry racket of a football game blares through the house.

Fragrances grow richer and more intense, in the dramatic tempo of a play. Lids tap dance beneath their nodding plumes of steam. The turkey is growing nut-brown and crackles to your fork.

Small fry keep flat-nosed vigil at the window, watching for company. "They're here, they're here!"

"I saw them first, I'll open the door!"

Aprons are whisked off, fires turned lower. "Now, boys—"

Greetings ring out. Relatives and friends swarm in.

"Everything's about ready. Children, wash your hands. Boys, get chairs to the table—"

Loved ones sit down together, bow their heads. "Dear Father, we thank Thee—"

Fireplace in den. Photograph by Jessie Walker

A GRAND THANKSGIVING

Terry Kay

In the extended rite of passage—from child to adult to senior citizen—my home is now the Thanksgiving gathering place for my children and grandchildren, which means my wife and I are no longer forced to do split-time traveling between family homes. Now, our children have that duty—a few hours in one place, a few hours more in another. It's part of a ritual for millions of people across America, like a national game of fruit-basket turnover.

But knowing they will be there matters. Truth is, I like the anticipation of the day almost as much as the day itself. I make daily trips to the grocery, having with me a cookbook that stays balanced on the childseat of the cart for emergency reference. I like meandering down aisles, plucking a this or a that from shelves on the chance I'll need whatever it is. I like the ticklish joy I get from giving in to whims on those excursions. (The whims are always related to grandchildren. Little surprises. Little things that say, "I didn't forget.")

I like the day-ahead cooking, especially when one or more of the grandchildren come early to stay the night and find some adventure in helping (a great word for a two-year-old) with the preparation. They stand on footstools, wearing tied-up aprons, and make pretend cakes in aluminum pans. They jabber incessantly, happily. I like the jabber. It has the sound of a spirited symphony. I like the pretend cakes. They taste of fruit and honey.

I also like when they get older and are tall enough to stand shoulder-to-shoulder beside me and I can give them tasks that require some attention and skill (scallion chopping, mashing potatoes, peeling carrots). My own young sous-chefs.

I like when they say, "Papa, you cook the best chicken in the world." I like knowing that if I cook it, they will come. Actually, that's not it. Not exactly. It should be: if they come, I will cook it. That's the power of their persuasion over me.

Over the river and through the wood,
To Grandfather's house away!
We would not stop for doll or top,
For 'tis Thanksgiving Day.
—Lydia Maria Child

Romantically, metaphorically, it's a bit like the parable of the Prodigal Son, which, to me, is the most perfect story in all of the world's literature.

They have been away, these children and grandchildren, and now they are returning home out of a great wish, or need, to be there. It is time to prepare the fatted calf and all that goes with it—time for celebration, time for giving thanks.

Nothing is as grand.

And it is the way I want to be remembered.

FATHER, WE THANK THEE

Peter Marshall

Father, we around this table thank Thee:

    For Thy great gift of life,

    That Thy love for us is not dependent

        upon any worthiness of ours,

    For good health,

    That we know neither hunger nor want,

    For warm clothes to wear,

    For those who love us best,

    For friends whose words of encouragement

        have often chased away dark clouds,

    For the zest of living,

    For many an answered prayer,

    For kindly providences that have

        preserved us from danger and harm.

We thank Thee that still we live in a land bountifully able to supply all our needs, a land which still by Thy Providence knows peace, whose skies are not darkened by the machines of the enemy, whose fields and woodlands are still unblasted by the flames of war, a land with peaceful valleys and smiling meadows still serene.

Oh, help us to appreciate all that we have, to be content with it, to be grateful for it, to be proud of it—not in an arrogant pride that boasts, but in a grateful pride that strives to be more worthy.

In Thy name, to whose bounty we owe these blessings spread before us, to Thee we give our gratitude. Amen.

A Thanksgiving Day dinner. Photograph by Jessie Walker

An Old-Time Thanksgiving

Wilbur D. Nesbit

The best of old Thanksgiving Day
    Was when the night came creeping down
And flung its veils of misty gray
    Above the countryside and town;
And windows glimmered here and there
    All suddenly against the dark,
While from the chimneys through the air
    Leaped many a cheery, friendly spark;
And then around the big fireplace
    The family sat circle-wise—
The blaze reflecting in each face
    And dancing in the children's eyes.

Oh, that was best, that twilight time,
    With nuts and apples on the hearth;
The stately hall clock's solemn chime
    Took on an overtone of mirth;
The old cat in contentment purred;
    The dog chased rabbits in his sleep;
A squirrel at the window chirred;
    And then the silence grew more deep,
Until we all were sitting there
    And watching how the embers turned
To palaces all high and fair,
    As into coals the backlog burned.

I hear it now—the clock's dull tick,
    The wind that sang among the trees,
The front gate's lazy whine and click
    As it was shaken by the breeze.
And how the stars marched up the sky—
    The mystic army of the night,
Each peering from its journey high
    Down through our window, at our light,
The old-time carpet, and the chairs,
    The shadows dancing on the wall,
The glinting railing of the stairs,
    The wraps heaped up out in the hall.

Then thanks were given for the day,
    The thanks that started from the heart;
And each of us was sure, some way,
    That he of goodness had a part.
And then, while play-tired children slept,
    The older folk talked gently on
Of golden memories they had kept
    As treasures of the days agone,
Until the grandsire, gray and tall,
    Began the song they must now know
And sang with smiles and led them all
    In "Praise God from whom all blessings flow."

The Little Things
Adam N. Reiter

Should you start to count your blessings
In the usual, offhand way,
Much like taking inventory
As of this Thanksgiving Day,
You'll no doubt list those outstanding
With a joy that thrills and clings;
But you'll have a happier total
If you count the little things.
Don't forget the smiling welcome
Of the ones you love so well,

Nor the peaceful evening hour
And the fireside's tranquil spell.
There are many, many blessings,
If we choose to count them all,
And it's only right to list them
With the source from which they fall;
So, when taking inventory,
Note the pleasure each one brings,
But be sure to make full entry—
Don't forget the little things.

Thanksgiving Time
Edna Jaques

I'm thankful for so many things;
It's hard to pick out just a few
And tell in little simple words
How very much they mean to you.

First there is sunlight, rich and warm,
Shining upon the house and lot;
The good laws of our native land,
For which our fathers lived and fought;

For neighbors just beyond the fence,
Whose lives are closely linked with ours,
With whom we share so many things—
Driveways and lights and growing flowers.

For crops of grain—for fruit and meat;
The fragrance of the earth, the trees;
Churches and schools and country lanes;
I am so thankful for all these;

And for children in a hundred schools;
For timid old folks, bent and worn;
Young mothers brave as knights of old,
Waiting for babies to be born;

For old church bells that softly chime;
A turkey at Thanksgiving time.

Otsego County, Michigan. Photograph by Darryl R. Beers

Everyday Mercies

Pamela Kennedy

When I was a young girl, I couldn't quite figure out why Thanksgiving was such a big occasion. Dad hauled home a huge turkey, Mom fretted over pumpkin and mincemeat pies, and Grandma whipped up a batch of her famous candied yams. My aunts and uncles and cousins showed up hefting covered dishes of their holiday specialties, and things pretty much focused around the dinner table—a big one for the adults and a smaller one for us children. Everyone ate way too much, and after dinner the women always ended up in the kitchen discussing the latest family crisis, while the men debated the importance of defense and offense as they hunkered around the television.

At school we made construction-paper turkeys, drew pictures of Pilgrims, and reviewed the story of the First Thanksgiving, which, I learned, wasn't very much like ours.

At church, we sang "Come, Ye Thankful People, Come" and "We Gather Together," which always left me wondering what it meant to be "chastened and hastened." The pastor enjoined us to be more grateful and less greedy, a message that left me with a twinge of guilt that never seemed to last long enough to prevent me from grabbing the last drumstick and an extra piece of pie.

The day after Thanksgiving was what I waited for. I was filled with anticipation as we headed for downtown Seattle department stores decorated as extravagant winter wonderlands and an opportunity to sit on Santa's lap to personally deliver my carefully prepared wish list. That, I thought, was much more exciting than overeating, cutting out paper Pilgrims, and singing hymns. I felt pretty secure back then. Gratitude didn't seem all that important. Wasn't life supposed to be good and filled with promises of even better things to come?

So many things change with time. Growing up, we all eventually learn, is more than just passing from one season to the next, ticking off holidays on the calendar. Experiences come along, both good and bad, and slowly childish assumptions are replaced with grown-up realities. We understand that wonderful things don't just fall into our laps, but that our hard work and determination, our patience and diligence are sometimes blessed and we succeed.

We find someone special to love and our hearts flood with amazement when we learn they love us back. We witness miracles like newborn babies and healed relationships; we forgive and are forgiven and discover that victory often comes after failure and that we are stronger than we knew. Our paradigms shift and one day we recognize that maybe life isn't supposed to be good, but sometimes it is anyway.

That's when Thanksgiving begins to become meaningful. That's when gratitude wells up within us, and we wonder at the everyday mercies all around us. Each new sunrise is occasion for thanks, and every starry night fills us with gratefulness.

On that first Thanksgiving in Plymouth, the Pilgrims and their Native American neighbors realized what each of us needs to learn: that being alive is all about being thankful. The winter had been hard. Their losses were devastating. Yet Providence had provided corn, and game, and abundance from the sea, with neighbors to help and a land in which

to be free. The pattern they set is affirmed each year when we gather together with family and friends around tables laden with traditional fare.

Our family circles expand and contract, our hearts beat in new and different cadences, we celebrate success and endure failure, but our need to celebrate Thanksgiving remains the same. All through the year there are times when we whisper quiet words of thanks for blessings small and large, but on Thanksgiving there is opportunity for collective and communal hymns of praise. And together we can echo the words of the ancient Psalmist.

Psalm 100

Make a joyful noise unto the Lord, all ye lands.
Serve the Lord with gladness: Come before his
   presence with singing.
Know ye that the Lord he is God: it is he that hath
   made us, and not we ourselves; we are his
   people, and the sheep of his pasture.
Enter into his gates with thanksgiving, and into
   his courts with praise: be thankful unto him,
   and bless his name.
For the Lord is good; his mercy is everlasting;
   and his truth endureth to all generations.

Stafford, Connecticut. Photograph by William H. Johnson

With Happy Hearts
Elizabeth Weaver Winstead

November leaves come tumbling down
To sweep the cloud-gray sky;
And from the empty cornfield rows,
The bronze-tipped pheasants fly.

Ripe apples hang from kitchen walls,
And squash reflects sun-mellowed days.
Gold pears adorn the orchard trees;
Warm firesides glow with shining blaze.

Large pumpkins line the roadside patch;
Brown fields hold stacks of ripened hay.
We celebrate this heritage
And bless Thanksgiving Day.

Our treasure day of harvest feast
Is shared with those we cherish best;
With happy hearts, we bow our heads
In praise and gratitude expressed.

No Word Has Failed
Grace Noll Crowell

Seedtime and harvest, cold and heat,
As long as the earth remains;
Seedtime and harvest, sun and wind,
And the warm sweet summer rains;
Over and over since time began
We've proved Thy faithfulness to man.

Lord, help us to thank Thee as we should
For this, Thy constant care:
For the good wheat for our daily bread,
For the outdoor pure, clean air;
For the fruits of garden, field, and tree
That tell anew Thy constancy.

Back of all these we see Thy hand
Opened to every need;
We see Thy might and mercy, Lord,
In each small jewelled seed;
May we walk with singing hearts of praise
Through all Thy glowing, golden days.

Waupaca County, Wisconsin. Photograph by Darryl R. Beers

Thanksgiving

Frances R. Havergal

Thanks be to God! to whom earth owes
    Sunshine and breeze,
The heath-clad hill, the vale's repose,
    Streamlet and seas,
The snowdrop and the summer rose,
    The many-voiced trees.

Thanks for the darkness that reveals
    Night's starry dower;
And for the sable cloud that heals
    Each fevered flower;
And for the rushing storm that peals
    Our weakness and Thy power.

Thanks for the sweetly-lingering might
    In music's tone;
For paths of knowledge, whose calm light
    Is all Thine own;
For thoughts that at the Infinite
    Fold their bright wings alone.

Yet thanks that silence oft may flow
    In dewlike store;
Thanks for the mysteries that show
    How small our lore;
Thanks that we here so little know
    And trust Thee all the more!

Thanks for the gladness that entwines
    Our path below;
Each sunrise that incarnadines
    The cold, still snow;
Thanks for the light of love which shines
    With brightest earthly glow.

Thanks for Thine own thrice-blessed Word,
    And Sabbath rest;
Thanks for the hope of glory stored
    In mansions blest;
Thanks for the Spirit's comfort poured
    Into the trembling breast.

Come Ye Thankful People, Come

Henry Alford

Come, ye thankful people, come,
Raise the song of harvest home;
All is safely gathered in,
Ere the winter storms begin;
God, our Maker, doth provide
For our wants to be supplied;
Come to God's own temple, come;
Raise the song of harvest home!

All the world is God's own field,
Fruit unto His praise to yield;
Wheat and tares together sown,
Unto joy or sorrow grown;
First the blade, and then the ear,
Then the full corn shall appear;
Lord of harvest, grant that we
Wholesome grain and pure may be.

Great Smoky Mountains National Park, North Carolina.
Photograph by Carr Clifton

THANKS FOR THE HARVEST
Laura Ingalls Wilder

The season is over, the rush and struggle of growing and saving the crops is past for another year, and the time has come when we pause and reverently give thanks for the harvest. For it is not to our efforts alone that our measure of success is due, but to the life principle in the earth and the seed, to the sunshine and to the rain—to the goodness of God.

We may not be altogether satisfied with the year's results, and we can do a terrific amount of grumbling when we take the notion. But I am sure we all know in our hearts that we have a great deal for which to be thankful. In spite of disappointment and weariness and perhaps sorrow, His goodness and mercy does follow us all the days of our lives.

As the time approaches when we shall be called upon by proclamation to give thanks, we must decide whether we shall show our thankfulness only by overeating at the Thanksgiving feast. That would seem a rather curious way to show gratitude—simply to grasp greedily what is given!

When a neighbor does us a favor, we show our appreciation of it by doing him a favor in return. Then when the Lord showers favors upon us, how much more should we try to show our gratitude in such ways acceptable to Him, remembering always the words of Christ, "Inasmuch as ye have done it unto one of the least of these my brethren, ye have done it unto Me" (Matthew 25: 40).

Whitefield, New Hampshire.
Photograph by William H. Johnson

Giving Thanks
Inez Franck

The table now is spread with luscious food,
The turkey browned, the golden pumpkin pie;
The family gathers round to say their thanks
For daily bread and gifts that glorify—

The mountain roads with scarlet-painted leaves,
The grain-filled barns, the harvest-glowing fields,
The roadside stands with apple cider poured,
The jams and jellies from the orchard yields.

This holiday is time for gratitude,
When sunlit kitchens wear red pepper strings
And coming home is blessed with memories
Of love and warmth and Mother's olden things.

Oh, let us bow in reverence to our Lord
And share the Pilgrims' faith, their precious will;
Among the autumn bounty, know He cares
And always helps our anxious dreams fulfill.

Thanksgiving Hymn
Author Unknown

O Thou, whose eye of love
Looks on us from above,
Low at Thy throne
We come to Thee and pray
That, gleaning day by day,
Our grateful hearts always
Thy hand may own.
Thine are the waving fields,
Thy hand the harvest yields;
And unto Thee,
To whom for rain and dew

And skies of sunny blue
Our love and praise are due,
We bend the knee.
And when beneath the trees
In fairer field than these
Our glad feet roam,
There where the bright harps ring,
May we our gleanings bring
And in Thy presence sing
Our harvest home.

Giving Thanks
Author Unknown

For the hay and the corn and wheat that is reaped;
For the labor well done, and the barns that are heaped;
For the sun and the dew and the sweet honeycomb;
For the rose and the song, and the harvest brought home—

Thanksgiving! Thanksgiving!

For the trade and the skill and the wealth in our land;
For the cunning and strength of the workingman's hand;
For the good that our artists and poets have taught;
For the friendship that hope and affection have brought—

Thanksgiving! Thanksgiving!

For the homes that with purest affection are blest;
For the season of plenty and well-deserved rest;
For our country extending from sea to sea,
The land that is known as the "Land of the Free"—

Thanksgiving! Thanksgiving!

Concord, Massachusetts.
Photograph by Dietrich Leis Photography

Every Day Thanksgiving
Harriet Prescott Spofford

Sweet it is to see the sun
    Shining on Thanksgiving Day;
Sweet it is to see the snow
    Fall as if it came to stay;
Sweet is everything that comes,
    For all makes cheer, Thanksgiving Day.

Fine is the pantry's goodly store,
    And fine the heaping dish and tray;
Fine the church bells ringing; fine
    All the dinners' great array,
Things we'd hardly dare to touch
    Were it not Thanksgiving Day.

Dear the people coming home,
    Dear glad faces long away;
Dear the merry cries; and dear
    All the glad and happy play.
Dear the thanks, too, that we give
    For all of this Thanksgiving Day.

But sweeter, finer, dearer far
    It might be if on our way,
With love for all, with thanks to Heaven,
    We did not wait for time's delay,
But with remembered blessings then
    Made every day Thanksgiving Day.

And the children of New England,
If they feast or praise or pray,
Should bless God for those brave Pilgrims
And their first Thanksgiving Day.
—Author Unknown

Oconto County, Wisconsin. Photograph by Darryl R. Beers

A Prayer of Thanks

Walter Rauschenbush

O God, we thank You for this earth, our home;
For the wide sky and the blessed sun;
For the salt sea and the running water;
For the everlasting hills and the
    never-resting winds;
For trees and the common grass underfoot.

We thank You for our senses
By which we hear the songs of birds,
And see the splendour of the summer fields,
And taste of the autumn fruits,
And rejoice in the fall of snow,
And smell the breath of spring.

Grant us a heart wide open to all this beauty;
And save our souls from being so blind
That we pass unseeing when even
The common thornbush is aflame with
    Your glory,
O God our creator,
Who lives and reigns forever and ever. Amen.

ISBN 0-8249-1310-8

Published by Ideals Publications
A Guideposts Company
535 Metroplex Drive, Suite 250
Nashville, Tennessee 37211
www.idealsbooks.com

Printed and bound in the U.S.A.
Printed on Weyerhaeuser Lynx. The paper used in this publication meets the minimum
requirements of American National Standard for Information Sciences—Permanence of
Paper for Printed Library Materials, ANSI Z39.48-1984.

Cover photograph: Autumn's bounty. Photograph by Dietrich Leis Photography
Inside front cover: AUTUMN EXCURSION. Painting by Richard Hook
Inside back cover: CEDAR WAXWINGS. Painting by Joan Beringer Pripps

ACKNOWLEDGMENTS

BORLAND, HAL. "The Traditions" from *Twelve Moons of the Year.* Copyright © 1979 by Barbara Dodge Borland as executor of the estate of Hal Borland. "The Thanksgiving Turkey" from *Sundial of the Seasons.* Copyright © 1964 by Hal Borland and renewed © 1992 by Donal Borland. Excerpts used by permission of Frances Collin, Literary Agent. CHRISTMAN, LANSING. "A Morning of Thanksgiving" from *Harp Strings in the Wind.* Copyright © 1998 by Lansing Christman and Nancy Ogle. Used by permission of Gayle McCants (POA for Lansing Christman). CROWELL, GRACE NOLL. "No Word Has Failed" from *Let the Sunshine In.* Copyright © circa 1970 by the author. Used by permission of Fleming H. Revell division of Baker Book House. FISHER, AILEEN. "Thanksgiving Day in the Morning" from *Ideals Thanksgiving* 1964. Used by permission of Marian Reiner on behalf of the Boulder Public Library Foundation, Inc. GRIPPO, ROBERT M. and CHRISTOPHER HOSKINS. An excerpt from the Introduction from *Macy's Thanksgiving Day Parade.* Copyright © 2004 by the authors. Courtesy of Arcadia Publishing. GUEST, EDGAR A. "The Old-Fashioned Thanksgiving" and "Thanksgiving." Used by permission of M. Henry Sobell, III. HOLMES, MARJORIE. "Thanksgiving" from *Love and Laughter,* Doubleday, 1967. Used by permission of Dystel & Goderich Literary Management. JAQUES, EDNA. "Goin' Home" and "Thanksgiving Time" from *The Golden Road* by Edna Jaques. Copyright © 1953. Thomas Allen Ltd. Used by permission of Louise Bonnell. MARSHALL, PETER. "Father, We Thank Thee" from *The Prayers of Peter Marshall.* Copyright © 1949, 1950, 1951, 1954, renewed © 1982 by Catherine Marshall. Used by permission of Fleming H. Revell, a division of Baker Publishing Group. TABER, GLADYS. "Thanksgiving At Stillmeadow," taken from "Fall," from *Stillmeadow Sampler.* Copyright © 1959 by Gladys Taber. Reprinted by permission of Brandt and Hochman Literary Agents, Inc. WILDER, LAURA INGALLS. "Thanks for the Harvest, November 1921" from *Little House In the Ozarks: Rediscovered Writings of Laura Ingalls Wilder.* Copyright © 1991 by editor Stephen W. Hines. Thomas Nelson, Inc. Used by permission of the editor. Our sincere thanks to the following authors or their heirs, some of whom we were unable to locate, for material submitted or previously used in Ideals publications: Raymond Crippen, Inez Franck, P. F. Freeman, Terry Kay, Pamela Kennedy, Wilbur D. Nesbit, Helen Colwell Oakley, Gelia K. Parker, Walter Rauschenbush, Adam N. Reiter, Richie Tankersley, and Elisabeth Weaver Winstead. Every effort has been made to establish ownership and use of each selection in this book. If contacted, the publisher will be pleased to rectify any inadvertent errors or omissions in subsequent reprints.